ENJOY IT WHILE IT HURTS

Also by JonArno Lawson

Poetry (and aphorisms) for adults

Love is an Observant Traveller
Inklings
This (and That was That)
There Devil, Eat That

Poetry for children

The Man in the Moon-Fixer's Mask
Black Stars in a White Night Sky
A Voweller's Bestiary
Think Again
Old MacDonald Had Her Farm
Down in the Bottom of the Bottom of the Box

As editor

Inside Out: Children's Poets Discuss Their Work

Prose

(Contributor to) *The Chechens: A Handbook*

ENJOY IT WHILE IT HURTS

An edifying miscellany of quarrelsome quips, holiday oddities,
curious thoughts and apocalyptic melancholia.

JonArno Lawson

WOLSAK
& WYNN

Cover image: JonArno Lawson
Cover design: JonArno Lawson
Book design: Rachel Rosen
Author photograph: Amy Freedman
Typeset in Adobe Caslon Pro
Printed by Coach House Printing Company Toronto, Canada

The publisher gratefully acknowledges the support of the Canada Council for the Arts, the Ontario Arts Council and the Canada Book Fund.

Wolsak and Wynn Publishers Ltd.
280 James Street North
Hamilton, ON
Canada L8R 2L3

Library and Archives Canada Cataloguing in Publication

Lawson, JonArno, author
    Enjoy it while it hurts / JonArno Lawson.

Poems.
ISBN 978-1-894987-77-6 (pbk.)

    I. Title.

PS8573.A93E54 2013   C811'.54   C2013-905447-2

For my dear, dear wife, Amy

There is a tiny marine creature called the sea squirt, which, in the earlier part of its life, swims around like a tadpole. It has a brain and a nerve cord to control its movements. But, when it matures, it attaches itself to a rock and stays in one place like a plant. Thereupon it digests its own brain and nerve cord because it no longer has a use for them.

– Joe Griffin and Ivan Tyrrell, *Human Givens: A new approach to emotional health and clear thinking*

We must be kind to each other. One of us is the world.

– Robert Clark Yates, "Sister Family Home," *Sister ~ Family ~ Home*

CONTENTS

i. LITTLE THAT'S EDIBLE

Little that's edible
Grows in a shade garden
A few incredible flowers
The rest are hardly flowers at all

Like leaves that tired
Of being leaves
And tried to flower –
If that's a bloom they failed to bloom.

It gets truly dark here first
where the light gets flummoxed
amongst plummeting stems
plunging down to some bedevilled
dunking in the dirt
It never really gets light
where there's never really been light

though something else was shed here
something darker than dark
that somehow renders the light inert.

ii. DANDELION QUEEN

Dandelion, in the stance of one stunned
or dream-drunk –
is stuck
standing stock-still
while her crown
gets lifted roughly in the wind's teeth
the wind
armless thief
tossing to the moist and furrowed
burglar earth
the Queen's furry jewels.

iii. SONG OF THE HOSTA

I'm hiding from the sun –
It tried to glimpse me from above
It burnt the grass while stalking me –
What was it thinking of?
Some wort said *heartless hosta*
But to me, that isn't love.

I saw I knew I understood
What couldn't be expressed
Its garment was a part of it
It couldn't be undressed.
It slunk around the throat
of what it festered, unconfessed.

The fat old sun, what's to be done?
Rays for fingers, flare for a thumb.

15

iv. PUFFBALL

The wind blew away my belly
The sun regrew my hair
"I'm proud I'm a cloud," I said out loud –
untrue – but I didn't care.

"…but you're not a cloud,"
coughed the mist as it bowed
down the hill it erased, unaware
of the sunlight it followed –
or that it was coughing
up spores it had swallowed.

v. A FOOLISH MOP OF BUSH

There was a foolish mop of bush
Brushed with red berries
Over which the wind cast
A loose net of sparrows
Who had no way of knowing
The thaw would be brief
That tomorrow their perch would be a lost fossil
Under a hovel of shuckling snow.

vi. TO ME IT SEEMS

To me it seems the ivy chokes slowly
But to the ivy the pace is perfect
Quick with its tendrils and fast, though calm, goes the ascent
Only if it meets another of its own kind do
Things become passionate
The embrace is to the death
Neither one able to reach up
Only to reach further and further along and around each other
Hopelessly entwined
Doomed to choke in the other's roots.

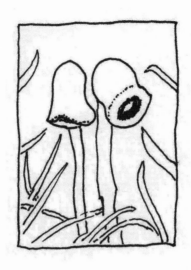

vii. ADVICE TO INDIAN PIPE

You keep going back to
where there's nothing left
acting vexed and upset
looking sad and perplexed –

But if you keep going back to
where you can't go back to
you'll never get to
where you might get next.

viii. GHOSTS OF A FLORAL MONARCHY

One brushes aside,
One banishes.
One blushes with pride,
then vanishes.

ix. MOUSE MOUTH

In the shade garden
A mouse mouth mops
Moths off the moss
While outside, bees in a pollen funk are stung
Into a yellow clutter by the sun's hot tongue

x. ORCHID IN A WINDOW

No need to switch the towels
for the orchid.
Its bath is the air
it dries there –
darling of higher powers
naked
and faking its flowers.

QUARRELSOME
QUIPS

(For Sophie, Ashey, and JoJo)

She who curses God Almighty
Drinking liquor in her nighty –
She's no flighty Aphrodite.

Those who know they know little, look down on those who confess
That compared to those who know little – they know even less,
While those who know they know nothing think nothing of it, I guess.

Those things that I've worn out,
Had first to be worn in,
Including my own skin.

Those who circle 'round with whips
with reddened eyes and frothing lips
aren't often calmed by comic quips.

Those who travel incognito and who fear the cruel mosquito
All share one important credo:
Don't go dancing in your speedo.

Those who always do their very best
May still at times wake up gravely depressed,
shedding bitter tears while getting dressed.

You, who've seen the circus and the zoo,
What good was either one of them to you?
They've caught and caged and tamed and trained you too.

Those who like things cut and dried
Often find they can't forget
The times they've wound up ripped and wet.

Those who've saved the best to last may feel that they've misused
Their past while those who've had the best at first
May wish they'd started with the worst.

You can't always free your mind from what's been written in your blood
But you can try a little harder – why sink back into the mud?
See now how those who danced for rain await their rescue from the flood.

Those who keep their wits about them
Don't try to get by without them
Listen to them – never doubt them.

Those who beat the midnight drums
Who sip champagne and savour plums
Aren't happy when the morning comes.

Those who treat themselves to more
Without once stopping to explore
Who else needs something, I deplore.

Those oppressed by city crowds
Should search for shipwrecks in the clouds
not mull dead prophets in their shrouds

Those who slave across the seas in dismal Asian factories
must marvel at the tawdry sleaze
of dollar-store democracies.

Those prompted then pre-empted by it
Called up then exempted by it
Are more confused than tempted by it.

Those who try to hurt themselves but find that nothing works
have had their fun and now they're numb – the force that fun exerts
has rendered them immune to pain (enjoy it while it hurts).

Those who clap to wake the dead
But wake the living up instead
Should keep their distance from my bed.

Addicted to the instantly accessible (. . .is that a crime?. . .)
Those whose appetites are irrepressible (. . .but not sublime)
Grope at thoughts they think are inexpressible (they're wrong, it just
takes time. . .)

Those who try, but find they can't turn
Off a light, that's hot but can't burn
Might have found a magic lantern.

The one who has bad dreams when sick saw
Some dream cowboy with a quick-draw chase a dandy in a rickshaw –
The cowboy's donkey bucked him – Hee-haw!

Those with a past that's faux pastiche
May still find themselves a niche
Amongst the nutbar nouveaux riches

Those who always get their way
Are tiresome to those who stay
Committed to means of fair play

You can lose a name or choose a name
Or use a name you stole:
The Nameless One won't know you by your name but by your soul.

Those who set their sights on things unseen
Unsettle those who try to read between
The lines that intersect the golden mean.

Those whose deeds go unreported,
And aren't allowed out unescorted
Likely feel unfairly thwarted.

Those who never get a word in
Edgewise may find it a burden
Leading lives they're never heard in.

The daring one who doesn't quite belong
Who's right – though no one sees it till she's wrong –
Sometimes gets remembered in a song.

The one who's endangered is too dull to mention
the one who's extinct gobbles all the attention:
On extinction lists your name persists.

Those who find their point of view
Is one you never listen to
may look for ways to injure you.

EXTINCT!...

ENDANGERED...

A guest arrived – inopportune
For those whose clothes were widely strewn
About the room that afternoon.

Those who treat life as a romp
Rarely go in for the pomp –
they snap their fingers, clap and stomp.

You who once loved me, why do you forsake me?
I'm not a bad habit –
you don't have to break me.

There's still light to lead you out, and there is light to save you:
Why are you searching in the dark
for someone to enslave you?

The self-made undertake themselves
With selfish plans they make themselves
Unreal, and then they fake themselves

Those who always jump the queue
Who leap the stile or hop the pew
Fare poorly under peer review.

He who walks on water can't dive down to the wreck
He must stretch out on the surface like a passenger on deck
To see your treasure he must strain his eyes, and crane his neck.

Those who steal successfully have often much rehearsed
This rule, to which good thieves adhere (in which they're all
       well-versed):
To avoid suspicion, rob your own house first.

Those who buckle down and brave the worst
Aren't often those who yell "I won!" "I'm first!" –
they know how quickly luck can be reversed.

Life can't be saved or reimbursed –
You've got to live it unrehearsed
Ditch your script, dive in headfirst!

Those who follow every kind of hype
Who eat the rotting fruit they're told is ripe
I don't need to describe – you know the type.

Those who find the words they need elusive
May find their search for perfect words conducive
To having thoughts unclear and inconclusive.

Those who sit in circles, twiddling thumbs
Waiting for what never, ever comes
Are lucky if there's padding for their bums.

Those who know the balconies (and who sang from them)
know those who know the shadows (and who sprang from them)
know those who know the ropes (and who to hang from them).

Those who do things bit by bit
Who take their time to match and fit,
By inner lights are often lit.

Those whose love is levity
Find humorous longevity
is best achieved through brevity.

Those the devil educates are clever
Their words and deeds may haunt the world forever
But are the devil-educated wise? Never.

Friend – abjure the ways of Pharaoh
Lay aside your bow and arrow
Bring the sun on your sombrero.

Those who have two halves to make a whole
Or halve the halves, if quarters are their goal
Have to have those halves under control

Three souls sit still to drink some soup
With others in their income group –
poor fool, lean dupe, thin nincompoop.

Three others start to make a racket
With other jackals in their snack bracket
Cunning clubber, rich weasel and greedy tweed jacket.

Only those who were seated succeeded
In finding a way to stand. Those who were standing already
Sat down again, feeling unsteady.

Those who come completely unprepared
But let their hearts direct them unimpaired
May achieve what others never dared

The fearless die along with the fearful:
A thought to make cowards
And pessimists cheerful!

Those who have the nerve but lack the knack
However great their verve for an attack
Best to keep them busy at the back.

Those who have the knack but lack the nerve
Who, when they see a problem, duck and swerve
Keep them, with the knackless, in reserve.

Those who pilfer filberts when they fish
Their fingers round the edges of my dish
May filch more filberts anytime they wish (I don't like them).

Those who squat down on their haunches
Lungs squashed up against their paunches
quickly knock themselves unconscious.

There are those who chase the devil,
And those the devil chases. But those who face the devil
Aren't the ones the devil faces.

Those who stood under understood
Their understanding would do no good
If nobody wondered where they stood.

Hard things are hard to say concisely
If you want to say them nicely. Hard to say
why that is, precisely.

There's really nothing quite so nice as
Being left to your own devices
With time to indulge every one of your vices

Those who spend their time and resources
Searching for, buying and raising racehorses
Don't waste their winnings at the racecourses.

When all of it's done, the grief and the fun,
and the light in my eyes finally dims,
I'll at least know what I did with my life was entirely based on my whims.

Why do you expect anyone to admire
That you're abstaining from
what you don't desire?

Those thoughts that arose
Out of your aroused mind – rotate them, deflate them
And leave them behind.

THE
FROG

AND   HIS

FOSTER

SON

(For my brother-in-law Mark, as promised)

A frog in a friar's frock
Came hopping through the fog
From lily pad to icy rock to water-sodden log
And by his side, his foster son
A one-time foundling pollywog –
(An orphan as the Chosen One must be) and
Worn out from the slog –
These two were on the run…

Furious fumed the friar –
"Oh why on earth did that frog require
The warmth of my only frock?
How on earth did it transpire
That I'd lose my frock to a frog?"
He shouted at his frightened dog
Who cowered by the fire.

The friar pulled on a sock and a boot
With one foot bare he hopped in pursuit
With his axe, out into the frost
But he might well have been in his birthday suit
For he lacked a good warm frock
(He'd also had too much grog) –
When he reached the edge of the endless bog
And hoisted his horrible axe
(though nowhere in sight was the frog…)
The North Wind stopped him dead in his tracks
As it blew up the legs of his burlap slacks
He cursed, and went stumbling back to his flat
Where he tripped on his frightened dog.

51

And sipping a last eggnog
While he wept and cursed the loss of his frock
He curled up and slept, bright red, on his back
And snored like a barnyard hog.

The Frog was as cold as ice
The webs of his feet were white
"I doubt," he said, to his foster son
"That I'll live through this frostbitten night
Even tucked up deep in the friar's frock
As snug as a foot in an old woollen sock
But you are the Chosen One –
You must finish what we've begun."

"Oh Lord, how I long for my lily-pad life
For the wind in the reeds
And my little green wife
With her comely croak, it cuts like a knife
To think that my time is done
That I'll never again see a pond
In spring
The hope that the flies and the pollywogs bring
The buzz and the bubbles and everything
That quickens the heart of a frog
Of a sentimental old frog."

"I'm sick of it, son, I'm sick of it
We've fallen far behind
And when I'm in the thick of it
I sometimes lose my mind!
The friar's so unforgiving,
So relentless and unkind!"

But his son said, "Father, be of good cheer
The earth still turns and daylight is near
And the friar you wronged lives close to here –
The time, my father, has come,
To undo the wrong that you've done
We must go and return the frock."

His father considered –
The field was littered
With signs of the grog-crazed friar –
The hopping footprints through the snow –
But from his window there came the glow –
and promise of a fire!

The father and son both gravely hopped
To the friar's door, and gently knocked
The friar, who answered, was greatly shocked
To see his heart's desire –
His one and only frock!

And behind it, trembling from the cold,
Two frogs – one young, and the other one old –
Sat ready to hear him rant and scold
Both were ready, in short, to expire.

But the holiday spirit took hold
And melted the heart of the friar:

"It augurs well, it augurs well
Auspicious are the signs
Exquisite are the dishes and
Delicious are the wines
And lucky you are, my little green friends
Who've come this morn to dine –
You have come, I hope, to dine?"

And so they all were reconciled
The dog wagged his tail,
And the weather grew mild
The friar, and the frog whom he'd once reviled
Sat arm in arm and croaked and smiled
Thanking their good-hearted foster child –
The orphaned Chosen One
Who'd finished what – come to think of it now –
Should never have really begun.

CURIOU THOUGHT

FOR BETH DARLING- TON

(for Beth Darlington)

The unfamiliar wakens (the familiar weakens) the urge to improvise.

Avoid being taught what's best learned by accident.

To either accept or reject an award is to take it too seriously.

What's oddest about the immodest: those who need modesty most badly boast madly.

Living means accepting the bad with the good, but why confuse them?

Some things are even more what they seem than they seem.

Trying to live up to the hopes and expectations of children would be more than enough to turn most of us into adults, which is the main reason that most adults prefer the company of adults.

Death is the last thing I want to experience.

People who hate people love people who hate themselves.

It is impossible to allow the weak their tyrannies without treating the vulnerable with contempt.

Have faith in what civilizes you.

While it's possible to pay attention to two people at once, it isn't possible that those two people will believe it's possible.

Disturb people's expectations all you want, but why destroy their hope?

It's funny that something as bright as a star spends all of its time in the dark.

The wise, in contrast to the clever, show no desire to be in a minority position.

The job for every present person is to leave behind a future.

If we can speak, we are wrong to let others speak for us, but just because we can speak, are we really always capable of speaking for ourselves?

Remember, you will be judged by the one foolish thing you say – not by your ten thousand sensible silences.

Catharsis is not a synonym for justice.

Proof of the dangers of not having schooling is that schools were invented by people who didn't have schooling.

Even the oldest and most reassuring traditions are, without exception, experiments.

You used to be somebody I knew; now you're just somebody I know.

Take the advice you would give yourself if you weren't yourself.

Everybody wants to put their batteries into beauty but nobody wants to read the instructions.

Don't put it on if you can't pull it off.

Things of no importance never happen.

"I'll believe it when I see it" is okay. "I'll perceive it when I see it" is better.

To create hope you will find that it's necessary to undertake tasks that seem hopeless.

There's too much to make sense of, and too much that doesn't make sense. And the more you look into things, in even the most casual way, the more there is of both.

Thankfully, most people are so appalling that it isn't necessary to feel any pity for them. Unfortunately, this doesn't free us from any annoying compulsion to be patient or merciful.

Love is the one experience that can return a person to a state of innocence. All other experiences serve only to divide us by making us believe in the importance of ourselves as separate from one another.

Those who aren't willing to do a bit of everything in general end up doing nothing.

You will save yourself much time forgiving and forgetting if you stop taking offence.

When someone does something important, it's hard for people to imagine that that person, with a bit more effort, might have done something even more important.

The most effective traps are the ones you don't realize you're in – this one, for instance.

Few of us notice what it is we've made central as a consequence of what we've marginalized.

If money could buy freedom from greed I'd do everything I could to make more of it.

Fight for – never against, never with.

The one who can't change changes everything.

The farther you go from something, the clearer it becomes what your connection to it is.

Trusting your instincts doesn't obligate you to act on them.

The more self-aware you become, the less self-conscious you'll be.

Was it from watching other animals that had learned to copy other animals that we learned to copy other animals?

Enemies are an incredibly exciting luxury that no one can really afford.

The only strength that matters is the strength you utilize to struggle with your weaknesses. All other strengths become, in time, forms of weakness.

An inability to deal with the reality of rejection inevitably leads to a rejection of reality.

The best thing someone old can teach you is how to listen to someone young.

Don't do twice for no one what you can do once and for all.

You love when things go your way – but not when things go your way without you.

To discover the real value of literature is to simultaneously become aware of the worthlessness of words.

DIVIDE AND CONQUER

In the current world things change so quickly that those who divide no longer have sufficient time to conquer. Instead, there is constant division, and smaller and smaller groups are briefly controlled in succession by an ever-larger number of tyrants.

Not surprisingly, the self internalizes all these tyrants, and divides itself accordingly. As a result, instead of enriching those around us with a varied, but unified, personality, we disrupt the lives of those closest to us with our thousand different slavish and tyrannical faces.

IT'S HARD TO LOSE

It's hard to lose your beauty
It's hard to lose your gold
It's hard to lose the one
who you once held but can't now hold.

It's hard to lose your patience
It's hard to lose your mind
It's hard to lose the one you finally found
But can't now find.

It's hard to lose the favour
you didn't have to earn
It's hard to lose your flavour
It's hard to lose your turn

It's hard to lose your *savoir faire*
It's hard to lose the race
It's hard to lose your privacy
It's hard to lose your place

It's hard to lose your sidekick
It's hard to lose your touch
It's hard to lose your knack, your nerve
your courage and your crutch.

It's hard to make a living
It's hard to fake your death
It's hard to be forgiving
When you're running out of breath

It's hard to do your duty
It's hard to be twice told
It's heaven to perceive all that you've held
in what you hold.

MY BUM

On November 15th I published my bum
It won the Big Bummer
And the little bum-bum
It was a bestseller
Everyone wanted my bum

My bum became instantly recognizable
Some went to spank it, others to kick it
but most critics adored it – the reviews said
"What a butt!" "A rousing rump!" "Extraordinary buns!" I felt uneasy.
What was happening to my bum? What had my backside become?

I always knew you had it in you –
why did you sit on it so long?
asked my dad
I never knew you had it in you,
I thought you flew by the seat of your pants
said my mum.

Later, almost too late, I realized
not everyone has a bum –
and you can't find the answers
if you haven't sought 'em
and you can't reach the top
if you don't have a bottom.

WHAT YOU COVET

What you covet –
Will you love it
Once you've got it?

Long you sought it
Though you thought it
Never really could be yours

Now it's yours –
your heart soars!
Down it crashes…

Hopes fulfilled
are murdered wishes –
longing gutters in the ashes.

Dreaming while you wash the dishes
Restless your attention switches
To your unpursued ambitions

Longing sparks
ignites and flashes –
unlived life remains delicious…

FOLLOWER AND LEADER

Why does everyone study the Leader? Leaders are easy to recognize, and in that sense, if necessary, easy to avoid. The Leader is nothing without followers. It is the Follower we must be wary of.

Note this – nobody fears being led, but nearly everybody fears being followed.

THE GIRL FOR ME

The crows are fat from eating snails
The ocean's fat from eating whales
The wind's a belly in my sails
And you're the girl for me

The day is fat with things undone
I've grown too fat to stand or run
But you're a lean and hungry one
And you're the girl for me.

You're not the one for me said she
Fat or skinny or fancy-free
Whoever you are it's not to be
you're not the man for me

She said to my face –
"I see."
I saw,
so I said, "I see…"

So I sailed away to a faraway shore
where a faraway girl at a faraway door
said your pride isn't something that's mine to restore
said that faraway girl to me.

The sun goes crashing into the waves
the dead sit up in their watery graves –
Salacia's servants and Neptune's slaves –
But never on land nor in sea was there ever a girl for me.

THE YOUNG MASTER

"Look up to the heavens, embrace the momentous,
my dear young master!" said the old apprentice.
"Keep your eyes on the road and avoid a disaster,
my dear old apprentice," replied the young master.

THE LITTLE RED HEN

I'm sick to death
Of that Little Red Hen
Asking for help
Again and again

Keep your damned bread
Gorge till you sicken –
I prefer feasting
On a well-fed chicken.

YOUR INTERESTS

It may seem paradoxical, but the most interesting thing to investigate is nearly always why something doesn't interest you.

LOVE, THOMAS JEFFERSON–STYLE, ANNAPOLIS, 1776

I bought a woman at the port –
My heart became involved.
I sold her in the marketplace –
Another problem solved.

HOW DID HE KNOW

How did he know to speak
Who'd often been thought too weak?
He grabbed at his tongue,
And worked it out,
He panicked is how,
The freak.

LOVE ME MORE

Love me more – no, not like that –
Not the way you love the cat –
You know what I'm getting at –
Pull me closer, push me flat.

THE LANGUAGE OF DREAMS

The majority of the world's languages are spoken only in one specific geographical location and time zone. This means that the majority of people who speak that language are usually asleep at the same time. The implications of this are interesting. All those who speak that language together by day are dreaming in it together by night.

It could be said that for six to eight hours a day, the language undergoes a complete transformation in its usage to a dream language. In contrast, a language like English or French is spoken and dreamed in by millions of people twenty-four hours a day. If minds influence each other in unknown ways, this may be causing a worldwide restlessness, a kind of psychic and linguistic insomnia.

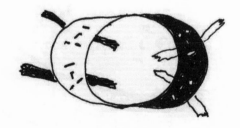

SPUR AND CURB

Spur yourself, accept the curb
No need to let harsh words perturb
Home truths should not disturb
Curb yourself, accept the spur
Stop stopping what you can't defer
See yourself as who you'll be
Accept yourself as you once were.

REFLECTIONS FROM CRATES, CYNIC OF THEBES

Come with me
To scold the whores
Old men in tunics
scarred by wars
Are sitting by
the city walls
Fixing nets
by empty seas

It's too late now
to settle scores
The whores have scaled
the city walls
Not one of them is scared to fall
Into the empty sea.

Old men with nets
they knot in shadows
Spitting olive pits
through gaps
Reproach lost wives
suggested by
The laughing waves
that warm their laps.

OLD MONKEYS

Like an old monkey I went in search of old monkeys I'd known long ago
Whose intimacies I'd welcomed and abandoned
Whose chests I'd beaten as I'd beaten my own
Old monkeys whose noses I'd broken and whose ears I'd bitten

I pursued the memories of these old monkeys for much longer
Than I'd pursued these actual monkeys when young
But here I was wanting to see them again
On the other end of a lifetime of considering what had happened
briefly between us

Long ago, up in the branches
Or down against the trunks
The fruitless pelting of the fruit which, apparently,
We should have eaten.

It all happened – all of it – just as you would imagine.
God help me let go of their hairy paws and run from this itching need
To forgive and be forgiven. I want to fight them again for the first
        time, and this time
to forget them completely after I pummel them away from me forever.

THE ABRAHAMIC SITUATION: JUDAISM, CHRISTIANITY & ISLAM

The dynamics are so family-like, and each one has been shaped to a large extent by its sibling-order and where "Dad" was working at the time:

You can almost hear them at a therapy session (Chris to Judy) "Well, you were born just after Dad was reposted from Egypt to Palestine, but I grew up in Rome, so my life was completely different – the clothes! – and Mom was around more then. And then to go from Rome to Mecca! I thought I'd die – it ruined my adolescence, but Dad insisted. He didn't care what it did to me. And that's where you were born, of course, Issy. Life was never the same after that."

DELIVER YOUR LOVER

Deliver your lover
A letter by ladder
You'll anger her mother
(her mum doesn't matter)

And later you'll leave her
Another love letter
To tell her you left her
The letter you left her

About how you'd leave her
If you ever found her
With some other lover
Because though you love her

You're frightened when leaving her
Sooner or later
That she'll discover
That she loves another

And so to be safe
You've decided to leave her. . .
"Oh brother," she'll mutter
"Another dud lover."

THE SNOW

The snow, like humanity,
Was most beautiful
Right after
It had fallen.

THROUGH THE GRASS BARKING

We all see the glass as
both half-full
and half-empty:
for most half is plenty.

Is it half-empty, half-full
or is the glass twice as large as it needs to be?
That the glass might be the problem
is welcome news to me.

Is the glass half-empty half as bad as
or no better than
the cup overflowing?
There's no way of knowing.

Either through a glass darkly
or through the grass barking
A great wagging tail whacks
the problem off smartly.

THE TAILORS AND THE BUTCHER

In all the excitement about the expulsion from the garden of Eden, two events are often overlooked. First, Adam and Eve sewed themselves loincloths out of leaves. Much is made of the fig leaves of course, but little is made of the fact that they invented sewing on the spot. It might be supposed that in this pre-metallurgic time, and before they had access to bones, they must have used wood splinters to sew, or perhaps they made little holes by hand and pushed tree fibres through. This, however, is the first example of human labour. They do this sewing before they are expelled and told they'll have to labour by the sweat of their brows to live. The first labour of humanity was to sew undergarments in paradise.

It is not surprising really that it was a feeling of embarrassment that led to the first labour.

The other line I want to draw your attention to, related to this one, is that God made them garments of leather. God did this. Note that God did not say, "Let there be leather pants." He did not create them. He made them. He also didn't wait for them to get dressed. He clothed them himself. Where did the skins come from? This important matter is skipped over quietly in the text. Did God make anything else anywhere in the Bible, or only the leather pants and jackets?

I wonder which of the beasts got slaughtered for its skin? It must have become instantly extinct, since breeding hadn't started yet, so we'll probably never know. Before Abel the shepherd and Cain the farmer came Adam and Eve the tailors and God the butcher.

THIS IS HOW IT STARTS

This is how it starts
This is how it ends
One learns all the parts
Another one pretends
One says, "Absolutely!"
Another, "It depends."

This is where it comes from
This is where it goes
One says, "Son, I'm certain"
Another, "No one knows."
The final curtain snags
while dragging back across your toes.

This is how to say it
This is what it means
Whichever way you play it
You play it out in scenes
The noblest nature fetched by need
out from its lousy genes
is not some sweet machinery –
we're nothing like machines.

A tethered punt sits bobbing in the cattails by the bank
You're given something precious there;
there's no one there to thank
Or is there always someone there
Of whom you're simply unaware?
A shadow rose and sank.

I DREW WHAT I HATED

I drew what I hated
I hid what I drew
I knew if I waited
I'd run into you
And you'd look in my eyes
And you'd know what I knew –
what I hid and I hated,
I knew if I waited
you'd know what to do –
you'd give me your hand
and you'd find a way through.

ACKNOWLEDGEMENTS TO THE BOOK OF JOB

The scroll maker came to tell Job that the skins were ready, and that a group of copyists had been employed. He was hoping that he might now have the final version to take away with him.

Job was almost finished. The story itself – a memoir, more or less – had been completed ages ago, but he'd been having some trouble with the acknowledgements:

"I'd like to thank my family for all of their suffering – they endured so much in the making of this story – but especially I'd like to thank Eliphaz the Temanite, Bildad the Shuhite and Zophar the Naamathite, who consoled and counselled me during difficult times. I bear no ill will towards the Sabeans or the Chaldeans, whom, I believe, acted without ill intent towards me."

He showed this to the scroll maker, and asked his opinion.

"Is it really necessary?" asked the scroll maker, "Your first family is dead – they'll never read this, nor will your enemies. Your friends actually gave you bad advice, remember? Do you really need to thank them?"

"They meant well," said Job.

The scroll maker shrugged.

"All right," said Job. "To hell with the acknowledgements."

"Any dedication?" asked the scroll maker.

"It's all dedication," said Job, "that's all it is."

MARIA THROUGH THE THORN FOREST GOING

Maria's legs were raked by thorns
God save our wretched souls
For seven years no child was born
Unkempt and untidy
Unwashed and unshorn
A dark figure moved through the bright yellow corn
Jesus, Jesus and Mary
What hope went dark in Mary's heart?
Kyrie eleison
To bear a child who'd never sin
Another step back and you'll never begin
Jesus Christ and Mary
Then in the brush
Where her legs were torn
A little babe to the girl was born
Too early to welcome, too late to warn
Christ alive and Mary.

THE THING IS

Things are doing things to you
You are doing things to things
To be being's to be doing
Doing things is to be renewing
What you are and what the thing is
What things are is worth reviewing
With every unfolding of your being
To be doing with your reviewing
Is to be pursuing the undoing
Of the overdoing of the overbearing
bringing of being
To the being of things.

(for Roald Hoffmann)

ROBOT BONES

I

The ship she was on had crashed
The others aboard had died
The hidden cameras we used to reconnoitre
Let us watch from inside on the monitor,
the searchlights searched,
then suddenly shone at her

Down in the quag of Cootes
In the paradisical quag
Where she strode through the mud in her lithium boots
Away from the burning ship

109

Nimbly avoiding rocks and roots –
Though she seemed to walk in a dream –
Nimbly but numbly, grim but agleam...
And the shadow she cast was iron black
As she passed in the light of the fiery stack
That stood by the old reactor

At once I could see that he longed to attract her
My tongue-tied tungsten friend
Her bewildered, fervent face
Shone into the lens as she got close –
He stood up to lower the shields that encroached
And with upraised hands
he now approached
The indecisive survivor
Of the blazing, molten ship.

She also raised her hands –

I watched them circle slowly
In a lachrymal pavan
As if I wasn't watching – as if I wasn't there
And then he laid his tungsten hand
Across her copper hair.

II

He brought her within the reactor
And led her down to the heavy water
Drenching her in fresh isotopes
By the blue glow of the core
Tending to her broken hopes
But still – there was something more
he had a compatible plug –
she leaned towards him
as if to hug
and he tried to give her his power.
But it wasn't any use.
Something in her was broken
Her outlets couldn't open.

III

She was the first to lose her power
We sat beside her that final hour
And when her time had come
When all the light had gone from her face
He said, "We've reached the end of the race
But it's death, not life, that will leave no trace
Of itself, when all's said and done.

For love is hungry and time is a crumb
Though I have no idea where she was from
love devoured our differences
and made of us a single sum...
I'd have liked a little more time..."
He glanced at her quiet face –
"I loved her brain's flerovium hum
And her skin of burnished molybdenum..."

IV

I swore an oath, a solemn oath,
that I would bury the bones of both,
side by side together,
in the crackling electrical undergrowth,
a final nest of red-hot wires to wrap them in their tomb.

I swore to him by the ozone layer
(back in those days, when it was still there),
and we both knelt down
for a digital prayer, while a fleeting memory saddened me
of his tungsten hand on her copper hair.

ACKNOWLEDGEMENTS

Noelle Allen, for the grant, and for her belief that a book could emerge from the first fragments I showed her. Paul Vermeersch, for his critical sympathy, and his very good ideas, and Ashley Hisson, for her careful copy-editing. Rachel Rosen, for her incredible design work.

Thanks to Barry Callaghan, for his editorial help with "The Tailors and the Butcher" – and to *Exile*, the literary quarterly, for first publishing it, a long, long time ago.

Parts of "The Frog and his Foster Son" appeared earlier as a poem commissioned by Abigail Richardson for the Toronto Symphony Orchestra in response to Osvaldo Golijov's *The Last Round*, published in the *Canadian Literary Review*. Several poems appeared in *Arc Poetry Magazine* 69, Fall 2012 (thanks to Katia Grubisic).

"Maria Through the Thorn Forest Going" is a very free reinvention of the German folk song "Maria durch ein Dornwald ging."

"Rob Your Own House First" was an idea expressed first by my daughter Sophie. Michael Joseph suggested that we see the half-empty/half-full cup both ways simultaneously.

I am grateful to David Pendlebury, who inspired "The Abrahamic Situation" and gave it its title. In response to this piece he said, "I picture 'Dad' sloping off to the garden shed to get some peace and quiet. Sometimes he wears a grin, sometimes an exasperated frown."

Thank you also to Sheila Barry, Michael Joseph, Charlene Diehl and Steven Heighton for their encouragement as I worked on the manuscript. Also, thanks to the good spirit of David Jones and his *In Parenthesis* and especially his *Anathemata*, which hover behind bits of "Robot Bones."

My children, Sophie and Ashey, did a brilliant job of illustrating an earlier version of the first section of this book. None of what I do would be possible without the love, support and inspiration of my dear wife, Amy, and our dear children, Sophie, Ashey and Joseph.

The idea for writing a sequence about a shade garden, where flowers might represent people, came from a conversation with the poet Soraya Peerbaye about her own shade garden.

My thanks to Ivan Tyrrell and Joe Griffin for permission to quote from their book, *Human Givens: A new approach to emotional health and clear thinking*. Chalvington, East Sussex: Human Givens Publishing, 2003. What a book!

Thanks also to Robert Clark Yates for permission to quote from his introductory essay, "Sister Family Home," from the anthology *Sister ~ Family ~ Home*, illustrated by Jason Avery, Fiona Kinsella, Paul Lisson. Clifford, ON: West Meadow Press, 1998.

The title design for "Shade Garden" was based on a title page design by Lewis F. Day. Many of the designs in the book are borrowed from the genius of (presumably) long-dead and (to me) nameless designers of books, bookplates, stone carvers, ornamental ironworkers, leather crafters and ceramicists.

JonArno Lawson is the award-winning author of numerous books of poetry for children and adults, including *Black Stars in a White Night Sky*, *A Voweller's Bestiary* and *Think Again*. A two-time winner of the Lion and the Unicorn Award for Excellence in North American Children's Poetry, he lives in Toronto with his wife and children.